7 Keys Workbook and Journal

A Companion to *Your Work, Your Life...Your Way*

Julie Cohen
Professional Certified Coach

ISBN: 978-0-9842474-1-7

Printed in the United States of America
First Edition

For Margaret—whom I miss every day.

Table of Contents

Thank you to the following people who helped me create this workbook and journal:

- Patty Enright, instructional designer, for her expertise in making the fieldwork work and her significant contributions to the 7 Keys book and workshops.
- Suzanne and Bob Murray of StyleMatters for their editorial and consulting services. It was so valuable to have two guides with me on the journey.
- Jerry Dorris of AuthorSupport.com for his creative talents and patience.
- Melissa Cohen for her unending design input and sisterly encouragement.
- My clients, who enable me to do the work I love.
- Nigel and Aaron—I love you guys!

Introduction

Congratulations on making a commitment to your journey toward a more satisfying, enriching, and meaningful work–life balance. This workbook and journal is an accompaniment to *Your Work, Your Life...Your Way: 7 Keys to Work–Life Balance* and can be used as your dedicated work space for completing all the fieldwork exercises in that book, as well as a place to record your thoughts and feelings as you delve deeper into the personal and professional challenges the book causes you to examine. There is also room here for you to reflect on your successes and learning as your lifelong journey toward work–life balance continues, beyond the reading of *Your Work, Your Life...Your Way*. Recording your reflections here will help you to see your progress, make adjustments on your direction, and celebrate your many accomplishments along the way. As with the book *Your Work, Your Life...Your Way,* while using the present workbook and journal you will be the primary "driver" in designing and implementing a more preferred way of working and living.

Throughout the book *Your Work, Your Life...Your Way*, you are provided with fieldwork exercises to help you become aware of how the 7 barriers to work—life balance may be getting in the way of your more preferred work—life balance and to help you integrate the 7 keys into your work and life. The present workbook/journal provides space to complete each of these fieldwork exercises and to record your related thoughts, ideas, brainstorms, and visions for the future. It is important to actually write the answers to each of the fieldwork exercises so that you can take them from your head and commit them to paper. There is power in making your ideas and plans concrete.

In *Your Work, Your Life...Your Way*, a graphic of a road sign with the word *Fieldwork* appears at the start of each fieldwork exercise, to indicate that you have come to a place in the book where pencil and paper are needed. Once you see this graphic, you will know to turn to the present workbook/journal to complete the corresponding exercise. At the start of each "chapter" in this workbook/journal, you will be asked to reflect on your strengths and growth areas related to a given key—these are bonus questions I have added to the workbook/journal, to help you further utilize your strengths and pinpoint areas where additional support and guidance may be beneficial. I have also included ample space in this workbook/journal to answer important questions that appear in *Your Work, Your Life...Your Way* and that invite you to go even deeper in looking at your work, your life, your choices, and the actions that can support you in creating a more satisfying mix of work and life priorities. These questions are referred to in this workbook/journal as "Key Reflections."

I encourage you to work through the fieldwork exercises in each chapter in the order in which they appear and to maintain a pace that feels both manageable (not adding any additional stress to your already busy life) and motivating. For change to happen, you need to commit time and energy to the exercises and to your experimentation with the new behaviors you are defining in the fieldwork exercises. Yet, as you work your way through the fieldwork, write journal entries, and record your own reflections, know that there are no prescribed time limits as to when you should complete each exercise.

At the end of each key-related chapter in this workbook/journal, I've also created "Going Deeper" questions that ask you to reflect on what you have learned from this process so far. This will help you quantify the benefits of the process to date and therefore encourage you to continue applying them in your life. As you answer these particular questions, you may also identify challenges and roadblocks you have encountered. Again, knowing this information will help you make better choices in the future.

Here are a few additional benefits of using this workbook and journal.

* You will have a consistent place to record your work so you will be able to see patterns, challenges, and progress.
* You can take this workbook/journal with you and record your thoughts, engage in exercises, and see your action plans regardless of where you are.
* You can revisit your plans and reflections as you and your life change. As highlighted in *Your Work, Your Life...Your Way*, work–life balance is a journey, not a destination. This workbook and journal can grow and change with you. You can add, redo, and redesign your solutions and plans as your life expands and evolves.

I have also included at the end of each workbook/journal chapter a few blank pages for each key, called "Additional Notes," where you can write down your general thoughts, learning, and observations on what matters most to you on this journey. Use these pages in whatever way you choose to support you in integrating that specific key into your life. For example, if you find yourself needing extra space to answer one of the questions in the workbook, feel free to turn to the back of the workbook/journal chapter and finish answering the question in the "Additional Notes" section. Or, perhaps, you will feel like writing a free-form journal entry on one of the topics raised in *Your Work, Your Life...Your Way*. The "Additional Notes" section can be a place for you to do this. You can also record questions and challenges there for which you need to seek support and answers from friends, family, colleagues, or your coach to keep you moving on your journey in your own way. This blank section at the end of each workbook/journal chapter is meant to be used in any way that supports you.

This workbook/journal is meant to assist you in creating more awareness of your work–life balance challenges and to help you focus on taking action to make real changes to move you closer to your desired mix of work and life. Congratulations on taking this step and enjoy the journey!

A Road Map for the Journey: How Satisfied Are You?

Identify Your Current Work–Life Balance Satisfaction

(see p. 21 in *Your Work, Your Life...Your Way*)

Today's Date: _____

Your Current Work–Life Balance Satisfaction Level (number between 1 and 10): ☐

How do you feel about this level (in three words or less):

_____

_____

Describe Your Preferred Work–Life Balance Situation

(see p. 23)

Describe your preferred work–life balance state—one in which the mix of your work and life priorities feels great to you. What does it look like? What does it feel like? How is it different from now? Write your comments, thoughts, and reflections.

_____

_____

_____

_____

_____

_____

_____

_____

_____

_____

_____

_____

_____

_____

_____

_____

_____

_____

_____

_____

Now, from your previous thoughts and reflections, create a concise descriptor in three words or less (hyphenated words are acceptable if you need them) so you have a clear and specific direction for your journey.

My compass is pointing toward _____ (write your three-word descriptor here).

The 7 Barriers and 7 Keys

Barrier	Key
1 – Problems With Prioritization	1 – Develop Priorities
2 – Lack of Boundaries	2 – Create Boundaries
3 – Inefficient Use of Time, Energy, and Attention	3 – Manage Your Day Efficiently
4 – Unreasonable Expectations	4 – Design Reasonable Expectations
5 – Incompatible Values	5 – Reprioritize Your Values
6 – Unbalanced Organizational Culture	6 – Navigate an Unbalanced Organizational Culture
7 – Lack of Self-Care	7 – Engage in Self-Care

KEY 1

Develop Priorities

Strengths and Growth Areas

? What do I do well in relation to setting priorities?

_____
_____
_____
_____
_____
_____
_____

? What are my challenges in relation to setting priorities?

_____
_____
_____
_____
_____
_____
_____
_____

Key Reflection

Who and what drives the selection of your priorities? Have you deliberately selected your work and personal priorities, or do you allow the natural course of your day and the people with whom you interact to dictate your priorities?

_____
_____
_____
_____
_____
_____
_____
_____
_____
_____
_____

If you are aware of your priorities, do you manage to maintain them most days or weeks, or are they continually falling by the wayside? What prevents you and what supports you in acting on them?

_____
_____
_____
_____
_____
_____
_____
_____
_____
_____
_____

Know What's Important

(see p. 34 in *Your Work, Your Life...Your Way*)

Use the following space to create your vision and/or record the themes of your vision (feel free to use additional paper if needed or to write in the "Additional Notes" section at the end of this workbook/journal chapter). Remember, your vision can be both personal and professional.

As a reminder, some possible methods for creating your vision include the following:

* imagine your future self
* design a vision board
* write a 2020 job description
* create a one, three, five, or ten-year plan.

My Vision

Key Reflection

Revisit the "Dealing With the Voice of the Critic" text box in *Your Work, Your Life... Your Way* (p. 34). As you think about your vision, how does the "gremlin," or a critical voice, pop into your head? What does it say? How does it impact the process of creating your vision?

_____

_____

_____

_____

_____

_____

_____

_____

_____

_____

Imagine a quiet gremlin. How do you move forward with your vision now? What's different? What do you need to do to lower the volume on your gremlin's voice?

_____

_____

_____

_____

_____

_____

_____

_____

_____

_____

_____

Know Your Priorities

(see p. 36)

From my vision, I have selected the following personal and professional priorities to focus on over the next six months.

Today's Date: _____

Over the next six months, I would like to accomplish these personal priorities:

   1. _____

   2. _____

   3. _____

   4. _____

Over the next six months, I would like to accomplish these professional priorities:

   1. _____

   2. _____

   3. _____

   4. _____

Special Considerations: As you choose your priorities, answer the following questions to help determine whether it is realistic that you can address these priorities right now.

* What will your financial resources allow in the next six months?
* What kind of time resources will you have to support these priorities in the next six months?
* What will your anticipated energy level in the next six months support?
* What adjustments are you ready and willing to make in your life to implement these priorities in the next six months?

After you answer these questions, revisit the priorities you have recorded in this exercise and make any appropriate adjustments.

What's Your Plan?
(see p. 41)

Complete the following statements.

Each day I will plan in this way:

_____

_____

_____

_____

_____

_____

_____

Each week I will plan in this way:

_____

_____

_____

_____

_____

_____

_____

Changes I need to make and/or support I need to get in order to integrate planning into my day and week are:

_____

_____

_____

_____

_____

_____

Key Reflection

How does low-priority creep impact you? Identify specific examples, as prompted below.
Identify examples of when you are in "reacting" mode:

_____

_____

_____

_____

_____

_____

_____

_____

Identify examples of when you are in "firefighting" mode:

_____

_____

_____

_____

_____

_____

_____

_____

Identify examples of when you are in "doing too much" mode:

_____

_____

_____

_____

_____

_____

_____

_____

Revisit p. 42 of *Your Work, Your Life...Your Way* and review some of the techniques for managing low-priority creep. They are also shown, in brief, below:

* create sacred time each day or each week for important work
* create a process for "triaging" emergencies
* create a list of projects that you are working on daily, weekly, and monthly
* set time aside daily and/or weekly for planning and strategic thinking.

How can you use these techniques, or others, to address the previous examples of low-priority creep you identified? What do you need to do differently? What support do you need? Use this space to brainstorm solutions and to create plan(s) to put into action for addressing low-priority creep in your own life.

Priorities in Action
(see p. 50)

Day 1, Date: _____

How did I implement my priorities today?

_____
_____
_____
_____
_____
_____
_____

Am I satisfied with what I accomplished today? Why or why not?

_____
_____
_____
_____
_____
_____
_____

What can I do differently tomorrow?

_____
_____
_____
_____
_____
_____
_____

Priorities in Action

(see p. 50)

Day 2, Date: _____

How did I implement my priorities today?

_____

_____

_____

_____

_____

_____

_____

Am I satisfied with what I accomplished today? Why or why not?

_____

_____

_____

_____

_____

_____

_____

What can I do differently tomorrow?

_____

_____

_____

_____

_____

_____

_____

Priorities in Action
(see p. 50)

Day 3, Date: _____

How did I implement my priorities today?

_____
_____
_____
_____
_____
_____
_____

Am I satisfied with what I accomplished today? Why or why not?

_____
_____
_____
_____
_____
_____
_____

What can I do differently tomorrow?

_____
_____
_____
_____
_____
_____
_____

Priorities in Action
(see p. 50)

Day 4, Date: _____

How did I implement my priorities today?

_____
_____
_____
_____
_____
_____
_____

Am I satisfied with what I accomplished today? Why or why not?

_____
_____
_____
_____
_____
_____
_____

What can I do differently tomorrow?

_____
_____
_____
_____
_____
_____

Priorities in Action
(see p. 50)

Day 5, Date: _____

How did I implement my priorities today?

_____
_____
_____
_____
_____
_____
_____

Am I satisfied with what I accomplished today? Why or why not?

_____
_____
_____
_____
_____
_____
_____

What can I do differently tomorrow?

_____
_____
_____
_____
_____
_____
_____

Priorities in Action
(see p. 50)

Day 6, Date: _____

How did I implement my priorities today?

_____
_____
_____
_____
_____
_____
_____
_____

Am I satisfied with what I accomplished today? Why or why not?

_____
_____
_____
_____
_____
_____
_____
_____

What can I do differently tomorrow?

_____
_____
_____
_____
_____
_____
_____

Priorities in Action

(see p. 50)

Day 7, Date: _____

How did I implement my priorities today?

_____
_____
_____
_____
_____
_____
_____

Am I satisfied with what I accomplished today? Why or why not?

_____
_____
_____
_____
_____
_____
_____

What can I do differently tomorrow?

_____
_____
_____
_____
_____
_____
_____

Going Deeper Questions

How does it feel to have a vision? How has having a vision impacted your priorities?

_____

_____

_____

_____

_____

_____

_____

_____

_____

_____

_____

_____

_____

What do you need to do to maintain your planning process? What could get in the way of doing so?

_____

_____

_____

_____

_____

_____

_____

_____

_____

_____

_____

_____

_____

What changes have you noticed now that you have implemented a planning process?

_____

_____

_____

_____

_____

_____

_____

_____

_____

_____

_____

_____

_____

_____

_____

_____

How did it feel to focus on your priorities? What is working well?

_____

_____

_____

_____

_____

_____

_____

_____

_____

_____

_____

_____

_____

_____

_____

What was the biggest challenge you faced when focusing on your priorities?

_____

_____

_____

_____

_____

_____

_____

_____

_____

_____

_____

_____

_____

_____

_____

What are you most proud of having accomplished in relation to your priorities?

_____

_____

_____

_____

_____

_____

_____

_____

_____

_____

_____

_____

_____

_____

_____

_____

Additional Notes on Key 1: Develop Priorities

Additional Notes on Key 1: Develop Priorities

Additional Notes on Key 1: Develop Priorities

KEY 2

Create Boundaries

Strengths and Growth Areas

? What do I do well in relation to creating boundaries?

_____

_____

_____

_____

_____

_____

_____

? What are my challenges in relation to creating boundaries?

_____

_____

_____

_____

_____

_____

_____

Key Reflection

To determine the areas in your life in which you are using boundaries right now, answer the questions below (if you need a reminder about what boundaries are, revisit p. 54 of *Your Work, Your Life...Your Way*).

Write down all the areas in your life where you are already good at maintaining boundaries. At work? With your spouse or partner? With your children? In your volunteer commitments? With your friends?

_____

_____

_____

_____

_____

_____

_____

_____

_____

_____

_____

_____

_____

_____

_____

_____

_____

_____

_____

_____

_____

_____

_____

_____

_____

What allows you to keep boundaries in these areas?

_____
_____
_____
_____
_____
_____
_____
_____
_____
_____
_____
_____
_____

How can you transfer this practice of maintaining boundaries to other important areas of your life?

_____
_____
_____
_____
_____
_____
_____
_____
_____
_____
_____
_____
_____
_____
_____
_____
_____

Identify Your Loose and Absent Boundaries

(p. 61 in *Your Work, Your Life...Your Way*)

Loose or Absent Boundary #1:

_____

_____

_____

Feeling and Impact:

_____

_____

_____

_____

_____

_____

_____

Loose or Absent Boundary #2:

_____

_____

_____

Feeling and Impact:

_____

_____

_____

_____

_____

_____

_____

_____

Loose or Absent Boundary #3:

_____

_____

_____

Feeling and Impact:

_____

_____

_____

_____

_____

_____

_____

Loose or Absent Boundary #4:

_____

_____

_____

Feeling and Impact:

_____

_____

_____

_____

_____

_____

_____

_____

_____

Loose or Absent Boundary #5:

_____

_____

_____

Feeling and Impact:

_____

_____

_____

_____

_____

_____

_____

_____

Loose or Absent Boundary #6:

_____

_____

_____

Feeling and Impact:

_____

_____

_____

_____

_____

_____

_____

_____

Key Reflection

What new, firm boundaries do you need to create in order to be able to maintain all the meaningful priorities you generated for yourself in the previous chapter? What loose boundaries do you need to tighten in order to move toward your ideal work–life balance?

_____

_____

_____

_____

_____

_____

_____

_____

_____

_____

_____

_____

_____

_____

_____

_____

_____

_____

_____

_____

_____

_____

_____

_____

_____

_____

_____

Creating Firm Boundaries

(see p. 66)

For each corresponding loose or absent boundary you have previously listed, create a firm, SMART Boundary. As a reminder, SMART boundaries are those that are...

- **S**pecific – you can clearly define the action or lack of action you will take
- **M**easurable – you can quantify the boundary and are aware when you are or you are not doing it
- **A**ttainable – you can actually do it; it is feasible to implement this boundary
- **R**ealistic – you believe you can uphold it; it is not unmanageable or unreasonable
- **T**ime-based – you define it within a time frame.

Firm, SMART Boundary #1:

_____

_____

_____

_____

How will I implement this new boundary?

_____

_____

_____

_____

_____

_____

What do I need to do differently to maintain this boundary?

_____

_____

_____

_____

_____

_____

To whom do I need to communicate this new boundary? What do I need to say?

_____

_____

_____

_____

_____

_____

_____

Firm, SMART Boundary #2:

_____

_____

_____

_____

How will I implement this new boundary?

_____

_____

_____

_____

_____

_____

_____

_____

What do I need to do differently to maintain this boundary?

_____

_____

_____

_____

_____

_____

_____

To whom do I need to communicate this new boundary? What do I need to say?

_____

_____

_____

_____

_____

_____

_____

Firm, SMART Boundary #3:

_____

_____

_____

_____

How will I implement this new boundary?

_____

_____

_____

_____

_____

_____

_____

What do I need to do differently to maintain this boundary?

_____

_____

_____

_____

_____

_____

_____

To whom do I need to communicate this new boundary? What do I need to say?

_____

_____

_____

_____

_____

_____

Firm, SMART Boundary #4:

_____

_____

_____

_____

How will I implement this new boundary?

_____

_____

_____

_____

_____

_____

_____

What do I need to do differently to maintain this boundary?

_____

_____

_____

_____

_____

_____

To whom do I need to communicate this new boundary? What do I need to say?

_____

_____

_____

_____

_____

_____

Firm, SMART Boundary #5:

_____

_____

_____

_____

How will I implement this new boundary?

_____

_____

_____

_____

_____

_____

_____

What do I need to do differently to maintain this boundary?

_____

_____

_____

_____

_____

_____

To whom do I need to communicate this new boundary? What do I need to say?

_____

_____

_____

_____

_____

_____

Firm, SMART Boundary #6:

_____

_____

_____

_____

How will I implement this new boundary?

_____

_____

_____

_____

_____

_____

_____

What do I need to do differently to maintain this boundary?

_____

_____

_____

_____

_____

_____

_____

To whom do I need to communicate this new boundary? What do I need to say?

_____

_____

_____

_____

_____

_____

_____

Choose one of your newly defined firm, SMART boundaries, one that will give you the most satisfaction to enact. Over the next week, test out this new boundary, using the plan you designed to implement it.

Answer the following questions about this newly implemented firm, SMART boundary.

How do you feel as you maintain this boundary?

_____

_____

_____

_____

_____

_____

_____

_____

_____

_____

What benefits are you gaining from maintaining this boundary?

_____

_____

_____

_____

_____

_____

_____

_____

_____

_____

When you are comfortable maintaining this new boundary, choose another from your list and revisit the same process of boundary-maintaining, followed by reflection, until you have implemented all of the desired boundaries from your list. More blank space for reflecting on additional boundaries is shown in the pages that follow.

Next firm, SMART boundary:

How do you feel as you maintain this boundary?

_____

_____

_____

_____

_____

_____

_____

_____

_____

_____

_____

_____

_____

What benefits are you gaining from maintaining this boundary?

_____

_____

_____

_____

_____

_____

_____

_____

_____

_____

_____

_____

_____

_____

_____

_____

Next firm, SMART boundary:

How do you feel as you maintain this boundary?

_____

_____

_____

_____

_____

_____

_____

_____

_____

_____

_____

_____

What benefits are you gaining from maintaining this boundary?

_____

_____

_____

_____

_____

_____

_____

_____

_____

_____

_____

_____

Next firm, SMART boundary:

How do you feel as you maintain this boundary?

_____

_____

_____

_____

_____

_____

_____

_____

_____

_____

_____

_____

_____

What benefits are you gaining from maintaining this boundary?

_____

_____

_____

_____

_____

_____

_____

_____

_____

_____

_____

_____

_____

Next firm, SMART boundary:

How do you feel as you maintain this boundary?

_____
_____
_____
_____
_____
_____
_____
_____
_____
_____
_____
_____
_____
_____

What benefits are you gaining from maintaining this boundary?

_____
_____
_____
_____
_____
_____
_____
_____
_____
_____
_____
_____
_____
_____
_____

Key Reflection

Define Your "Buckets" (see p. 73 for more information on this technique)

In what ways do you want to spend your time? Identify the activities that are important to you and that you want to protect:

Bucket #1 _____

Bucket #2 _____

Bucket #3 _____

Bucket #4 _____

Bucket #5 _____

Bucket #6 _____

Bucket #7 _____

Bucket #8 _____

How does it feel to have identified your buckets?

_____

_____

_____

_____

_____

_____

How does your answer to the previous question support you in maintaining your priorities?

_____

_____

_____

_____

_____

_____

Key Reflection

Tighten Up, Then Lighten Up (see p. 74)

Where can you incorporate the "tighten up, then lighten up" strategy?

_____

_____

_____

_____

_____

_____

_____

_____

_____

_____

_____

_____

_____

What do you need to consider and remember as you experiment with this new approach?

_____

_____

_____

_____

_____

_____

_____

_____

_____

_____

_____

_____

_____

After you have implemented the strategy, record the benefits of using "tighten up, then lighten up."

_____

_____

_____

_____

_____

_____

_____

_____

_____

_____

_____

Going Deeper Questions

What was your initial comfort level when thinking about boundaries? How do you feel now? What has made a difference?

_____
_____
_____
_____
_____
_____
_____
_____
_____
_____
_____
_____

How have others reacted to your firm boundaries?

_____
_____
_____
_____
_____
_____
_____
_____
_____
_____
_____
_____
_____
_____

What support do you need to maintain your boundaries?

_____
_____
_____
_____
_____
_____
_____
_____
_____
_____
_____
_____
_____

What benefits have you gained from implementing new boundaries and/or making current boundaries firmer?

_____
_____
_____
_____
_____
_____
_____
_____
_____
_____
_____
_____
_____
_____
_____

Moving forward, how do you want boundaries to be part of your work and your life?

_____

_____

_____

_____

_____

_____

_____

_____

_____

_____

_____

How will you use your awareness of your "buckets" to uphold your boundaries? What support do you need to do this?

_____

_____

_____

_____

_____

_____

_____

_____

_____

_____

_____

_____

_____

Additional Notes on Key 2: Create Boundaries

Additional Notes on Key 2: Create Boundaries

Additional Notes on Key 2: Create Boundaries

KEY 3

Manage Your Day Efficiently

Strengths and Growth Areas

? What do I do well in relation to managing my day efficiently?

_____

_____

_____

_____

_____

_____

? What are my challenges in relation to managing my day efficiently?

_____

_____

_____

_____

_____

_____

Identify Your Leaks

(see p. 88 in *Your Work, Your Life...Your Way*)

Over the next week, look for areas in your work or personal life where you are experiencing leaks in your day. Be as detailed as possible, describing when the leak occurred, what you were doing, how it felt, and the impact. Leaks can include any of the following (plus a variety of types that are not shown here and may be unique to you):

* multitasking
* lack of planning
* no support structure
* no delegation
* clutter/messy office or workspace
* social networking black hole.

Leak #1: _____

Details:

_____

_____

_____

_____

_____

Leak #2: _____

Details:

_____

_____

_____

_____

_____

_____

Leak #3:
Details:

_____
_____
_____
_____
_____

Leak #4:
Details:

_____
_____
_____
_____
_____

Leak #5:
Details:

_____
_____
_____
_____
_____

Leak #6:
Details:

_____
_____
_____
_____
_____

Leak #7: _____

Details:

_____
_____
_____
_____
_____
_____

Leak #8: _____

Details:

_____
_____
_____
_____
_____
_____

Leak #9: _____

Details:

_____
_____
_____
_____
_____
_____

Leak #10: _____

Details:

_____
_____
_____
_____
_____

Design Your Own Plugs

(see p. 97)

For each of the leaks you identified in the previous exercise (*Identify Your Leaks* fieldwork), create a plug—a method to remedy the leak. Design small actions that you can do to lessen or stop the specific inefficiency or energy drain.

Remember the following:

* time box is a plug for multitasking
* planning time is a plug for lack of planning time
* get support is a plug for no support structure
* delegation is a plug for no delegation
* organize is a plug for clutter/messy office or workspace.

And, of course, you can also design your own plugs to address your unique leaks.

Plug #1 _____

Plug #2 _____

Plug #3 _____

Plug #4 _____

Plug #5 _____

Plug #6 _____

Plug #7 _____

Plug #8 _____

Plug #9 _____

Plug #10 _____

Key Reflection

How do you feel about delegation? If you are challenged with the process of delegation, what false messages or beliefs get in the way of you delegating to others?

_____

_____

_____

_____

_____

_____

_____

_____

_____

_____

_____

_____

_____

_____

_____

_____

_____

_____

_____

_____

_____

_____

_____

_____

_____

_____

_____

Create a Delegation Action Plan
(see p. 100)

Complete the following items.

Define the task you want to delegate:

_____

_____

_____

_____

Identify the person to whom you want to delegate the task:

_____

What does successful completion of this task look like? Be as specific as possible.

_____

_____

_____

_____

_____

_____

_____

When do you need the project completed and returned to you?

_____

Possible script for you to use when asking for delegation assistance:

_____

_____

_____

_____

_____

What can get in the way of you actually delegating the given task?

_____
_____
_____
_____
_____
_____

How can you overcome this possible roadblock to delegation?

_____
_____
_____
_____
_____
_____
_____

What will be the benefit of actually using delegation? (Consider the benefits to you, to the person with whom you are delegating, and to the organization.)

_____
_____
_____
_____
_____
_____

Make a commitment to using delegation by completing the following statement:

I will ask _____ to do _____
_____
for me and complete and return it to my by _____.

Plug Your Leaks

(see p. 102)

Select the first plug that you will put into action from the previous *Design Your Own Plugs* exercise. Be as detailed as possible, describing what you will do.

Plug I will implement:

_____

_____

After you implement your first plug, identify a positive result from making this change:

_____

_____

_____

_____

_____

_____

How did it feel to implement this first plug?

_____

_____

_____

_____

_____

_____

What worked well? What did not work well?

_____

_____

_____

_____

_____

_____

If appropriate, how do you need to change the plug for next time?

_____
_____
_____
_____
_____
_____

After you feel comfortable with the first plug you implemented, choose another. In each case, give yourself time and space to get used to the new behavior change and to observe the results.

Next plug I will implement:

_____

_____

After you implement this plug, identify a positive result from making this change:

_____

_____

_____

_____

_____

How did it feel to implement this plug?

_____

_____

_____

_____

_____

What worked well? What did not work well?

_____

_____

_____

_____

If appropriate, how do you need to change the plug for next time?

_____

_____

_____

_____

After you feel comfortable with this plug, choose another.

Next plug I will implement:

_____

_____

After you implement this plug, identify a positive result from making this change:

_____

_____

_____

_____

_____

How did it feel to implement this plug?

_____

_____

_____

_____

_____

What worked well? What did not work well?

_____

_____

_____

_____

If appropriate, how do you need to change the plug for next time?

_____

_____

_____

_____

After you feel comfortable with this plug, choose another.

Next plug I will implement:

_____

_____

After you implement this plug, identify a positive result from making this change:

_____

_____

_____

_____

_____

How did it feel to implement this plug?

_____

_____

_____

_____

_____

What worked well? What did not work well?

_____

_____

_____

_____

If appropriate, how do you need to change the plug for next time?

_____

_____

_____

_____

After you feel comfortable with this plug, choose another.

Next plug I will implement:

_____
_____

After you implement this plug, identify a positive result from making this change:

_____
_____
_____
_____
_____

How did it feel to implement this plug?

_____
_____
_____
_____
_____

What worked well? What did not work well?

_____
_____
_____
_____

If appropriate, how do you need to change the plug for next time?

_____
_____
_____
_____

After you feel comfortable with this plug, choose another.

Going Deeper Questions

What did you learn by observing your leaks?

_____
_____
_____
_____
_____
_____
_____
_____
_____
_____
_____
_____
_____

How did your behavior change just by being aware of your leaks?

_____
_____
_____
_____
_____
_____
_____
_____
_____
_____
_____
_____
_____

How did you feel when you created your own plugs?

_____

_____

_____

_____

_____

_____

_____

_____

_____

_____

_____

_____

_____

How did it feel to implement a plug?

_____

_____

_____

_____

_____

_____

_____

_____

_____

_____

_____

_____

_____

How has your perspective on delegation changed?

_____
_____
_____
_____
_____
_____
_____
_____
_____
_____
_____
_____
_____
_____

How do you want to integrate delegation in your future?

_____
_____
_____
_____
_____
_____
_____
_____
_____
_____
_____
_____
_____
_____
_____

Additional Notes on Key 3: Manage Your Day Efficiently

Additional Notes on Key 3: Manage Your Day Efficiently

Additional Notes on Key 3: Manage Your Day Efficiently

KEY 4

Design Reasonable Expectations

Strengths and Growth Areas

? What do I do well in relation to expectations?

_____
_____
_____
_____
_____
_____

? What are my challenges in relation to expectations?

_____
_____
_____
_____
_____
_____

Identify the Unreasonable Expectations of Others

(see p. 114 in *Your Work, Your Life...Your Way*)

Others' unreasonable expectation #1:

_____

_____

Impact:

_____

_____

_____

_____

Cause:

_____

_____

_____

_____

Others' unreasonable expectation #2:

_____

_____

Impact:

_____

_____

_____

_____

Cause:

_____

_____

_____

_____

Others' unreasonable expectation #3:

_____

_____

Impact:

_____

_____

_____

_____

Cause:

_____

_____

_____

_____

Others' unreasonable expectation #4:

_____

_____

Impact:

_____

_____

_____

_____

Cause:

_____

_____

_____

_____

Others' unreasonable expectation #5:

_____

_____

Impact:

_____

_____

_____

_____

Cause:

_____

_____

_____

_____

Identify Your Unreasonable Expectations of Yourself
(see p. 118)

Unreasonable expectation of myself #1:

_____

_____

Impact:

_____

_____

_____

_____

_____

Unreasonable expectation of myself #2:

_____

_____

Impact:

_____

_____

_____

_____

_____

Unreasonable expectation of myself #3:

_____
_____

Impact:

_____
_____
_____
_____
_____

Unreasonable expectation of myself #4:

_____
_____

Impact:

_____
_____
_____
_____
_____

Unreasonable expectation of myself #5:

_____
_____

Impact:

_____
_____
_____
_____

Key Reflection

Pay attention to your use of extreme language, such as "I must," "I should," or "I always." What patterns do you notice? When do you most speak or think thoughts containing these or similar phrases? How does this kind of thinking impact you?

_____

_____

_____

_____

_____

_____

_____

_____

_____

_____

_____

_____

_____

_____

_____

_____

_____

_____

_____

_____

_____

_____

_____

_____

_____

_____

_____

_____

Address Others' Unreasonable Expectations

(see p. 123)

Revisit the *Identify the Unreasonable Expectations of Others* exercise, and select one unreasonable expectation you would like to address.

What is the unreasonable expectation held of me that I would like to change?

_____

_____

_____

_____

_____

_____

_____

_____

_____

Who holds this unreasonable expectation of me?

_____

What exactly makes this expectation unreasonable to me?

_____

_____

_____

_____

_____

_____

_____

_____

_____

What might be a more reasonable expectation that I could propose?

_____

_____

_____

_____

_____

_____

_____

_____

_____

_____

_____

_____

_____

How do I want to start this conversation? (Remember—use an "I" statement.)

_____

_____

_____

_____

_____

_____

_____

_____

_____

_____

_____

_____

_____

_____

_____

What reasons can I give to advocate for the new, shared, reasonable expectation?

Reason #1:

_____

_____

Reason #2:

_____

_____

Reason #3:

_____

_____

What would be the ideal result from this conversation?

_____

_____

_____

_____

_____

_____

How would my life change if we created a new, shared, reasonable expectation?

_____

_____

_____

_____

_____

_____

Revisit the *Identify the Unreasonable Expectations of Others* exercise, and select one unreasonable expectation you would like to address.

What is the unreasonable expectation held of me that I would like to change?

_____

_____

_____

_____

_____

_____

_____

_____

_____

_____

_____

Who holds this unreasonable expectation of me?

_____

What exactly makes this expectation unreasonable to me?

_____

_____

_____

_____

_____

_____

_____

_____

_____

_____

_____

_____

What might be a more reasonable expectation that I could propose?

_____

_____

_____

_____

_____

_____

_____

_____

_____

_____

_____

_____

How do I want to start this conversation? (Remember—use an "I" statement.)

_____

_____

_____

_____

_____

_____

_____

_____

_____

_____

_____

_____

_____

_____

_____

What reasons can I give to advocate for the new, shared, reasonable expectation?

Reason #1:

_____

_____

Reason #2:

_____

_____

Reason #3:

_____

_____

What would be the ideal result from this conversation?

_____

_____

_____

_____

_____

_____

_____

How would my life change if we created a new, shared, reasonable expectation?

_____

_____

_____

_____

_____

_____

_____

Revisit the *Identify the Unreasonable Expectations of Others* exercise, and select one unreasonable expectation you would like to address.

What is the unreasonable expectation held of me that I would like to change?

_____

_____

_____

_____

_____

_____

_____

_____

_____

_____

_____

_____

Who holds this unreasonable expectation of me?

_____

What exactly makes this expectation unreasonable to me?

_____

_____

_____

_____

_____

_____

_____

_____

_____

_____

_____

What might be a more reasonable expectation that I could propose?

_____
_____
_____
_____
_____
_____
_____
_____
_____
_____
_____
_____
_____
_____

How do I want to start this conversation? (Remember—use an "I" statement.)

_____
_____
_____
_____
_____
_____
_____
_____
_____
_____
_____
_____
_____
_____
_____
_____
_____
_____
_____

What reasons can I give to advocate for the new, shared, reasonable expectation?

Reason #1:

_____

_____

Reason #2:

_____

_____

Reason #3:

_____

_____

What would be the ideal result from this conversation?

_____

_____

_____

_____

_____

_____

_____

How would my life change if we created a new, shared, reasonable expectation?

_____

_____

_____

_____

_____

_____

_____

Reframe Your Own Unreasonable Expectations

(see p. 126)

Revisit the *Identify Your Unreasonable Expectations of Yourself* exercise. Create a more reasonable "reframe" for each unreasonable expectation.

Unreasonable expectation of myself #1:

_____

_____

More reasonable reframe:

_____

_____

_____

_____

_____

What I need to do differently:

_____

_____

_____

_____

When I will do it:

_____

_____

_____

_____

Unreasonable expectation of myself #2:

_____

_____

More reasonable reframe:

_____

_____

_____

_____

_____

_____

_____

What I need to do differently:

_____

_____

_____

_____

_____

_____

_____

When I will do it:

_____

_____

_____

_____

_____

_____

Unreasonable expectation of myself #3:

_____

_____

More reasonable reframe:

_____

_____

_____

_____

_____

_____

_____

What I need to do differently:

_____

_____

_____

_____

_____

_____

_____

When I will do it:

_____

_____

_____

_____

_____

_____

_____

Unreasonable expectation of myself #4:

_____

_____

More reasonable reframe:

_____

_____

_____

_____

_____

_____

_____

What I need to do differently:

_____

_____

_____

_____

_____

_____

When I will do it:

_____

_____

_____

_____

_____

_____

Unreasonable expectation of myself #5:

_____

_____

More reasonable reframe:

_____

_____

_____

_____

_____

_____

What I need to do differently:

_____

_____

_____

_____

_____

_____

When I will do it:

_____

_____

_____

_____

_____

_____

Key Reflection

Underpromise and Overdeliver: A Strategy to Set Reasonable Expectations in Advance (see p. 127)

How did you test out this strategy?

_____

_____

_____

_____

_____

_____

_____

_____

_____

_____

After you have engaged in the underpromise-and-overdeliver strategy, answer the following questions.

How did it feel to underpromise?

_____

_____

_____

_____

_____

_____

_____

_____

_____

_____

_____

How did it impact the way you accomplished the task?

_____
_____
_____
_____
_____
_____

How did it feel when you overdelivered?

_____
_____
_____
_____
_____
_____

What direct feedback did you receive regarding the completion of the task?

_____
_____
_____
_____
_____
_____

If you were satisfied with the benefit and results of underpromising and overdelivering, how do you want to further incorporate this strategy into your daily activities?

_____
_____
_____
_____
_____
_____

If you were not satisfied with underpromising and overdelivering, how might you tweak that process to work better for you?

_____

_____

_____

_____

_____

_____

_____

_____

_____

_____

_____

_____

_____

_____

_____

_____

_____

_____

_____

Going Deeper Questions

What did you notice about the unreasonable expectations that others have of you? How do these expectations impact you?

_____

_____

_____

_____

_____

_____

_____

_____

_____

_____

_____

What was it like to create a shared, reasonable expectation with someone else? What worked well for you? What was difficult for you?

_____

_____

_____

_____

_____

_____

_____

_____

_____

_____

_____

_____

_____

What did you notice about the unreasonable expectations that you have of your-self? How do they impact you?

_____

_____

_____

_____

_____

_____

_____

_____

_____

_____

_____

_____

_____

How did the process of reframing your own expectations feel? What did you learn from it?

_____

_____

_____

_____

_____

_____

_____

_____

_____

_____

_____

_____

_____

_____

How did it feel to underpromise and overdeliver? What results did you observe?

_____

_____

_____

_____

_____

_____

_____

_____

_____

_____

_____

_____

_____

_____

What new behaviors do you want to incorporate in order to keep all expectations more reasonable?

_____

_____

_____

_____

_____

_____

_____

_____

_____

_____

_____

_____

_____

_____

_____

_____

Additional Notes on Key 4: Design Reasonable Expectations

Additional Notes on Key 4: Design Reasonable Expectations

Additional Notes on Key 4: Design Reasonable Expectations

KEY 5

Reprioritize Your Values

Strengths and Growth Areas

? What am I very clear about in relation to my values?

_____

_____

_____

_____

_____

_____

? What are my challenges in relation to my values?

_____

_____

_____

_____

_____

_____

Name Your Values

(see p. 137 in *Your Work, Your Life...Your Way*)

Review this list and circle any values that feel meaningful and relevant to you. Add other values that do not appear on the list that are important to you.

Accomplishment	Design	Health
Accuracy	Devotion	Holiness
Acknowledgment	Directness	Honesty
Action	Discovery	Honor
Advancement	Education	Humor
Adventure	Elegance	Imagination
Aesthetics	Empathy	Independence
Art	Empowerment	Individuality
Attractiveness	Enlightenment	Influence
Authenticity	Excellence	Ingenuity
Beauty	Excitement	Innovation
Bliss	Exhilaration	Integrity
Certainty	Experience	Intimacy
Choice	Experimentation	Joy
Clarity	Expertise	Knowledge
Collaboration	Fame	Leadership
Commitment	Family	Lifelong-Learning
Community	Feelings	Loyalty
Compassion	Financial Security	Mastery
Connectedness	Flexibility	Meaning
Contribution	Freedom	Mentoring
Creativity	Fun	Moderation
Danger	Grace	Music
Daring	Harmony	Nature

Orderliness	Relationships	Superiority
Originality	Relaxation	Systems
Partnership	Religion	Teaching
Passion	Resilience	Tenderness
Peace	Responsibility	Thrill-Seeking
Perfection	Risk Taking	Time w/Family
Performance	Romance	and Friends
Persistence	Self-Expression	Tradition
Persuasion	Self-Sufficiency	Tranquility
Play	Sensuality	Trust
Pleasure	Serenity	Unity
Power	Service	Vitality
Prestige	Spirituality	Wellness
Productivity	Sports	Winning
Recognition	Strength	Zest
Refinement	Success	

Insert your own values here, as needed.

_____

_____

_____

_____

_____

_____

_____

_____

_____

_____

_____

_____

_____

Identify Your Core Values
(see p. 140)

Narrow your circled values from the list in the previous fieldwork (*Name Your Values*) to a "top ten" list of core values. As you engage in this narrowing process, feel free to combine two or three values together if they mean similar things to you and feel important at a core level.

My Ten Core Values

1. _____

2. _____

3. _____

4. _____

5. _____

6. _____

7. _____

8. _____

9. _____

10. _____

Key Reflection

How did it feel to select ten core values? What did you learn about yourself that was new? What did you remember about yourself that perhaps you had forgotten?

_____

_____

_____

_____

_____

_____

_____

_____

_____

_____

_____

_____

_____

_____

_____

_____

_____

_____

_____

_____

_____

_____

_____

Write Your Personal Values Statements
(see p. 141)

Complete the following to define what each of your ten core values mean to you.

1. _____ means this to me:

_____

_____

_____

_____

_____

_____

2. _____ means this to me:

_____

_____

_____

_____

_____

_____

3. _____ means this to me:

_____

_____

_____

_____

_____

_____

_____

4. _____ means this to me:

_____

_____

_____

_____

_____

_____

5. _____ means this to me:

_____

_____

_____

_____

_____

_____

6. _____ means this to me:

_____

_____

_____

_____

_____

_____

7. _____ means this to me:

_____

_____

_____

_____

_____

_____

8. _____ means this to me:

_____

_____

_____

_____

_____

_____

9. _____ means this to me:

_____

_____

_____

_____

_____

_____

10. _____ means this to me:

_____

_____

_____

_____

_____

_____

Key Reflection

Revisit p. 146 in *Your Work, Your Life...Your Way* to get more information on the common pitfalls that lead to incompatible values, shown below:

* golden handcuffs
* adrenaline junkie
* success equals feeling overwhelmed
* means to an end.

Which of these, or what other pitfalls, impact you and how?

_____

_____

_____

_____

_____

_____

_____

_____

_____

_____

_____

_____

_____

_____

_____

_____

_____

_____

_____

_____

Discover Your Incompatible Values
(see p. 148)

Think about the values you are living right now versus the values inherent in your desired work–life balance. Answer the following questions.

What dominating value(s) serve(s) as a barrier to your desired work–life balance?

Value #1:

_____

_____

Value #2:

_____

_____

Value #3:

_____

_____

What decisions do you make and actions do you take (or not take) that support this/ these dominating value(s)?

_____

_____

_____

_____

_____

_____

_____

_____

_____

_____

_____

What value(s) are you sacrificing in order to support the dominant value?

Value #1:

_____

_____

Value #2:

_____

_____

Value #3:

_____

_____

How might your desired work–life balance be supported by changing your behavior to reflect the "sacrificed" value?

_____

_____

_____

_____

_____

_____

_____

_____

_____

_____

_____

_____

_____

_____

_____

To Reprioritize or to Accept?

(see p. 157)

Describe the values reprioritization you will make and the accompanying behavior change.

Value Reprioritization #1:

From _____ to _____

Behavior Change:

_____
_____
_____
_____
_____
_____
_____
_____
_____
_____
_____
_____
_____

Value Reprioritization #2:

From _____ to _____

Behavior Change:

_____
_____
_____
_____
_____
_____
_____
_____
_____
_____
_____

Value Reprioritization #3:

From _____ to _____

Behavior Change:

_____
_____
_____
_____
_____
_____
_____
_____
_____
_____
_____

Going Deeper Questions

How do you feel now that you have defined your core values? What feels different in comparison to how you felt before you engaged in this exercise?

_____

_____

_____

_____

_____

_____

_____

_____

_____

_____

_____

How can you purposefully remain aware of your core values?

_____

_____

_____

_____

_____

_____

_____

_____

_____

_____

_____

_____

_____

How do you want to manage values incompatibilities that you discover?

_____
_____
_____
_____
_____
_____
_____
_____
_____
_____
_____
_____
_____
_____

What incompatibilities are you willing to accept?

_____
_____
_____
_____
_____
_____
_____
_____
_____
_____
_____
_____
_____
_____
_____
_____
_____

What are you not willing to sacrifice around your values?

_____
_____
_____
_____
_____
_____
_____
_____
_____
_____
_____
_____
_____

What support do you need for making the behavior changes for your newly reprioritized values?

_____
_____
_____
_____
_____
_____
_____
_____
_____
_____
_____
_____
_____
_____
_____

Additional Notes on Key 5: Reprioritize Your Values

Additional Notes on Key 5: Reprioritize Your Values

Additional Notes on Key 5: Reprioritize Your Values

Additional Notes on Key 5: Reprioritize Your Values

KEY 6

Navigate an Unbalanced Organizational Culture

Strengths and Growth Areas

? What is working well in my life in relation to the organizations to which I belong?

_____

_____

_____

_____

_____

_____

? What are my challenges in relation to the organizations to which I belong?

_____

_____

_____

_____

_____

_____

Key Reflection

Name the organizations of which you are a part.

1. _____

2. _____

3. _____

4. _____

5. _____

Other:

_____

_____

_____

_____

_____

_____

Evaluate Your Organizations

(see p. 170 in *Your Work, Your Life...Your Way*)

Consider each of the organizations to which you belong and answer the following questions for each.

Organization #1: _____

How does this organization sabotage my work–life balance preferences or not support them?

_____

_____

_____

_____

_____

What is the impact of this situation on me?

_____

_____

_____

_____

_____

Organization #2: _____

How does this organization sabotage my work–life balance preferences or not support them?

_____
_____
_____
_____
_____

What is the impact of this situation on me?

_____
_____
_____
_____
_____

Organization #3: _____

How does this organization sabotage my work–life balance preferences or not support them?

_____
_____
_____
_____
_____

What is the impact of this situation on me?

_____
_____
_____
_____
_____

Organization #4: _____

How does this organization sabotage my work–life balance preferences or not support them?

_____
_____
_____
_____
_____

What is the impact of this situation on me?

_____
_____
_____
_____
_____

Organization #5: _____

How does this organization sabotage my work–life balance preferences or not support them?

_____
_____
_____
_____
_____

What is the impact of this situation on me?

_____
_____
_____
_____
_____

Know Your Time Limits
(see p. 175)

Create time limits based on the number of hours you are willing to commit to your organizations. Begin by writing down the particular activity; then, write down the number of hours you would like to commit each week or month to that particular activity.

My work time limits:

_____ for no more than ___ hr/week or ___ hr/month

_____ for no more than ___ hr/week or ___ hr/month

_____ for no more than ___ hr/week or ___ hr/month

_____ for no more than ___ hr/week or ___ hr/month

_____ for no more than ___ hr/week or ___ hr/month

My home/family time limits:

_____ for no more than ___ hr/week or ___ hr/month

_____ for no more than ___ hr/week or ___ hr/month

_____ for no more than ___ hr/week or ___ hr/month

_____ for no more than ___ hr/week or ___ hr/month

_____ for no more than ___ hr/week or ___ hr/month

My other organizational time limits:

_____ for no more than ___ hr/week or ___ hr/month

_____ for no more than ___ hr/week or ___ hr/month

_____ for no more than ___ hr/week or ___ hr/month

_____ for no more than ___ hr/week or ___ hr/month

_____ for no more than ___ hr/week or ___ hr/month

Key Reflection

A Last Attempt: "Firing" Your Boss (see p. 178)

If you do decide that you are willing to leave the organization, map out your strategy for "firing" your boss by answering the following questions (if extra space is needed, you may also turn to the "Additional Notes" section at the end of this workbook/journal chapter).

What situation(s) in my organization am I no longer willing to accept, therefore I am ready to attempt to "fire my boss"?

_____

_____

_____

_____

_____

_____

_____

_____

_____

_____

How might I start this conversation with my boss? What do I want him/her to know?

_____

_____

_____

_____

_____

_____

_____

_____

_____

_____

What adjustments/changes do I need in my current organization in order to consider staying? If my boss was 100% responsive to my work–life balance concerns, what would change?

_____

_____

_____

_____

_____

_____

_____

_____

What changes at my employer are enough for me to stay and not "fire my boss"?

_____

_____

_____

_____

_____

_____

_____

_____

What is my Plan B if I do not get the results I want and do leave my organization?

_____

_____

_____

_____

_____

_____

_____

_____

Define Organizational Possibilities

(see p. 185)

Review the organizational challenges you identified in the *Evaluate Your Organizations* fieldwork. Define possible options for addressing these issues.

Organization #1: _____

What possibilities are there for addressing the organizational challenges to my desired work–life balance?

_____
_____
_____
_____
_____

How might I propose new ways of operating in and with my organization?

_____
_____
_____
_____
_____
_____

Organization #2: _____

What possibilities are there for addressing the organizational challenges to my desired work–life balance?

_____

_____

_____

_____

_____

How might I propose new ways of operating in and with my organization?

_____

_____

_____

_____

_____

Organization #3: _____

What possibilities are there for addressing the organizational challenges to my desired work–life balance?

_____

_____

_____

_____

_____

How might I propose new ways of operating in and with my organization?

_____

_____

_____

_____

_____

Organization #4: _____

What possibilities are there for addressing the organizational challenges to my desired work–life balance?

_____
_____
_____
_____
_____

How might I propose new ways of operating in and with my organization?

_____
_____
_____
_____
_____

Organization #5: _____

What possibilities are there for addressing the organizational challenges to my desired work–life balance?

_____
_____
_____
_____
_____

How might I propose new ways of operating in and with my organization?

_____
_____
_____
_____
_____

Key Reflection

As you think about taking action to address the unbalanced organizational culture(s) impacting you, how do you feel? What excites you? What concerns you?

_____

_____

_____

_____

_____

_____

_____

_____

_____

_____

_____

_____

_____

_____

_____

_____

_____

_____

_____

_____

_____

_____

_____

_____

_____

Take a First Step to Address an Unbalanced Organizational Culture

(see p. 190)

Select one organization from the previous *Define Organizational Possibilities* fieldwork and come up with a first step of action to address your concern. Complete the following items.

Organization: _____

I will take the following first step:

_____

_____

_____

_____

_____

My desired outcome of this step is:

_____

_____

_____

_____

_____

The support I need to take this step is:

_____

_____

_____

_____

_____

After you have taken the first step, answer the following questions:

How did I feel taking this step?

_____

_____

_____

_____

_____

What did I learn from this step?

_____

_____

_____

_____

_____

What is the next step I want to take?

_____

_____

_____

_____

_____

Continue this process until you are ready to stop and/or select another organization in which to take another first step toward change.

Organization: _____

I will take the following first step:

_____
_____
_____
_____
_____

My desired outcome of this step is:

_____
_____
_____
_____
_____

The support I need to take this step is:

_____
_____
_____
_____
_____

After you have taken the first step, answer the following questions:

How did I feel taking this step?

_____

_____

_____

_____

_____

What did I learn from this step?

_____

_____

_____

_____

_____

What is the next step I want to take?

_____

_____

_____

_____

_____

Continue this process until you are ready to stop and/or select another organization in which to take another first step toward change.

Organization: _____

I will take the following first step:

_____
_____
_____
_____
_____

My desired outcome of this step is:

_____
_____
_____
_____
_____

The support I need to take this step is:

_____
_____
_____
_____
_____

After you have taken the first step, answer the following questions:

How did I feel taking this step?

_____

_____

_____

_____

_____

What did I learn from this step?

_____

_____

_____

_____

_____

What is the next step I want to take?

_____

_____

_____

_____

_____

Continue this process until you are ready to stop and/or select another organization in which to take another first step toward change.

Organization: _____

I will take the following first step:

_____
_____
_____
_____
_____

My desired outcome of this step is:

_____
_____
_____
_____
_____

The support I need to take this step is:

_____
_____
_____
_____
_____

After you have taken the first step, answer the following questions:

How did I feel taking this step?

_____

_____

_____

_____

_____

What did I learn from this step?

_____

_____

_____

_____

_____

What is the next step I want to take?

_____

_____

_____

_____

_____

Continue this process until you are ready to stop and/or select another organization in which to take another first step toward change.

Organization: _____

I will take the following first step:

_____
_____
_____
_____
_____

My desired outcome of this step is:

_____
_____
_____
_____
_____

The support I need to take this step is:

_____
_____
_____
_____
_____

After you have taken the first step, answer the following questions:

How did I feel taking this step?

_____

_____

_____

_____

_____

What did I learn from this step?

_____

_____

_____

_____

_____

What is the next step I want to take?

_____

_____

_____

_____

_____

Continue this process until you are ready to stop and/or select another organization in which to take another first step toward change.

Going Deeper Questions

How will you know when it is time to take action or time to leave an organization?

_____
_____
_____
_____
_____
_____
_____
_____
_____
_____
_____
_____

What would enhance your ability to address organizational issues related to your work–life balance?

_____
_____
_____
_____
_____
_____
_____
_____
_____
_____
_____
_____
_____
_____

What amount of organizational imbalance is acceptable to you?

_____

_____

_____

_____

_____

_____

_____

_____

_____

_____

_____

_____

_____

What do you need to create a more balanced organizational culture within your family?

_____

_____

_____

_____

_____

_____

_____

_____

_____

_____

_____

_____

_____

_____

Who are your advocates in your organization(s)? How can they continue to support you in addressing your unbalanced organizational culture?

_____

_____

_____

_____

_____

_____

_____

_____

_____

_____

_____

_____

What fears are impacting your ability to take action to address an unbalanced organizational culture? How can you work through these fears and challenges?

_____

_____

_____

_____

_____

_____

_____

_____

_____

_____

_____

_____

_____

_____

Additional Notes on Key 6:
Navigate an Unbalanced Organizational Culture

Additional Notes on Key 6:
Navigate an Unbalanced Organizational Culture

Additional Notes on Key 6:
Navigate an Unbalanced Organizational Culture

Additional Notes on Key 6:
Navigate an Unbalanced Organizational Culture

KEY 7

Engage in Self-Care

Strengths and Growth Areas

?   What am I doing well in relation to my self-care?

_____

_____

_____

_____

_____

_____

?   What are my challenges in relation to self-care?

_____

_____

_____

_____

_____

_____

Where Are You Lacking?

(see p. 204 in *Your Work, Your Life...Your Way*)

Reviewing the past week, record the ways in which you did not take care of yourself.

	Date	Description
1.		
2.		
3.		
4.		
5.		
6.		
7.		
8.		
9.		
10.		

Impact of Current Self-Care Choices

(see p. 205)

For each item generated in the *Where Are You Lacking?* fieldwork, describe how that missed opportunity for self-care (that choice) impacted you and/or how it made you feel.

How my choices impacted me:

1. _____

2. _____

3. _____

4. _____

5. _____

6. _____

7. _____

8. _____

9. _____

10. _____

Key Reflection

What are your feelings and thoughts regarding your self-care activities? What have you discovered from completing the first 2 self-care exercises?

_____

_____

_____

_____

_____

_____

_____

_____

_____

_____

_____

_____

_____

_____

_____

_____

_____

_____

_____

_____

_____

_____

_____

_____

_____

_____

_____

_____

Revisit p. 207 in *Your Work, Your Life...Your Way* to review the four steps required for greater self-care. As a reminder, they are...

* commit time and energy
* put yourself first, at times
* stay clear on what matters to you
* surround yourself with a supportive environment.

Answer the following questions related to these steps.

How do you need to mentally reframe the idea of giving time to yourself? What will make it feel acceptable for you to create a small oasis of self-care time?

_____

_____

_____

_____

_____

_____

_____

_____

How do you want to feel when you are taking care of just yourself?

_____

_____

_____

_____

_____

_____

_____

_____

_____

_____

Who can you seek out to be your advocate, ally, supporter, or teammate in taking better care of yourself?

_____

_____

_____

_____

_____

_____

_____

_____

_____

_____

Designing Your Self-Care Prescription Plan
(see p. 211)

Short-Term Self-Care Choices

Describe ten daily or weekly activities, choices, or lack-of-activities that will enhance your self-care.

1. _____

2. _____

3. _____

4. _____

5. _____

6. _____

7. _____

8. _____

9. _____

10. _____

Longer-Term Self-Care Choices

Describe five monthly or annual activities or choices that will enhance your self-care.

1. _____

2. _____

3. _____

4. _____

5. _____

Key Reflection

How do you feel when reviewing the two self-care lists you created?

_____

_____

_____

_____

_____

_____

_____

_____

_____

_____

_____

_____

_____

_____

_____

_____

Ensuring Successful Self-Care
(see p. 214)

Benefits of Greater Self-Care

1. _____

2. _____

3. _____

4. _____

5. _____

Self-Care Implementation

First short-term self-care choice to implement:

_____
_____
_____
_____
_____

First longer-term self-care choice to implement:

_____
_____
_____
_____
_____

Observations regarding impact of these actions:

_____

_____

_____

_____

Second short-term self-care choice to implement:

_____

_____

_____

_____

Second longer-term self-care choice to implement:

_____

_____

_____

_____

Observations regarding impact of these actions:

_____

_____

_____

_____

Third short-term self-care choice to implement:

_____

_____

_____

_____

Third longer-term self-care choice to implement:

_____
_____
_____
_____

Observations regarding impact of these actions:

_____
_____
_____
_____

Fourth short-term self-care choice to implement:

_____
_____
_____
_____

Fourth longer-term self-care choice to implement:

_____
_____
_____
_____

Observations regarding impact of these actions:

_____
_____
_____
_____

Fifth short-term self-care choice to implement:

_____

_____

_____

_____

Fifth longer-term self-care choice to implement:

_____

_____

_____

_____

Observations regarding impact of these actions:

_____

_____

_____

_____

Going Deeper Questions

How did it feel after you were able to make some time for yourself and schedule something just for you?

_____

_____

_____

_____

_____

_____

_____

_____

_____

_____

_____

_____

What excuses and/or beliefs got in the way of your implementation of a self-care activity?

_____

_____

_____

_____

_____

_____

_____

_____

_____

_____

_____

_____

_____

_____

_____

What do you need to do, change, or shift in order to implement a new self-care activity?

_____

_____

_____

_____

_____

_____

_____

_____

_____

_____

_____

_____

_____

_____

_____

What support helped you implement a self-care choice?

_____

_____

_____

_____

_____

_____

_____

_____

_____

_____

_____

_____

_____

_____

_____

What do you need to continue doing in order to keep self-care a priority? What do you need to stop doing?

_____
_____
_____
_____
_____
_____
_____
_____
_____
_____
_____
_____
_____
_____

What excited you most about greater self-care?

_____
_____
_____
_____
_____
_____
_____
_____
_____
_____
_____
_____
_____
_____
_____
_____
_____

Additional Notes on Key 7: Engage in Self-Care

Additional Notes on Key 7: Engage in Self-Care

Additional Notes on Key 7: Engage in Self-Care

Additional Notes on Key 7: Engage in Self-Care

The Journey Continues: Taking Stock and Maintaining Momentum

Recap: The 7 Keys

Review your progress regarding each key and accompanying barrier in order to evaluate how you wish to continue working toward your more desired work–life balance.

Key 1: Develop Priorities

Progress I have made on this key:

_____

_____

_____

_____

_____

_____

_____

Progress I have made on this key (continued):

_____
_____
_____
_____
_____
_____
_____
_____
_____

Remaining challenges with this barrier (problems with prioritization):

_____
_____
_____
_____
_____
_____
_____
_____
_____
_____
_____
_____
_____
_____
_____
_____
_____

Key 2: Create Boundaries

Progress I have made on this key:

_____
_____
_____
_____
_____
_____
_____
_____
_____
_____
_____
_____
_____
_____
_____
_____
_____

Remaining challenges with this barrier (lack of boundaries):

_____
_____
_____
_____
_____
_____
_____
_____
_____
_____
_____

Key 3: Manage Your Day Efficiently

Progress I have made on this key:

_____
_____
_____
_____
_____
_____
_____
_____
_____
_____
_____
_____
_____
_____

Remaining challenges with this barrier (inefficient use of time, energy, and attention):

_____
_____
_____
_____
_____
_____
_____
_____
_____
_____
_____

Key 4: Design Reasonable Expectations

Progress I have made on this key:

_____
_____
_____
_____
_____
_____
_____
_____
_____
_____
_____
_____
_____
_____
_____
_____

Remaining challenges with this barrier (unreasonable expectations):

_____
_____
_____
_____
_____
_____
_____
_____
_____
_____
_____

Key 5: Reprioritize Your Values

Progress I have made on this key:

_____
_____
_____
_____
_____
_____
_____
_____
_____
_____
_____
_____
_____
_____
_____

Remaining challenges with this barrier (incompatible values):

_____
_____
_____
_____
_____
_____
_____
_____
_____
_____
_____

Key 6: Navigate an Unbalanced Organizational Culture

Progress I have made on this key:

_____
_____
_____
_____
_____
_____
_____
_____
_____
_____
_____
_____
_____
_____
_____
_____
_____
_____

Remaining challenges with this barrier (unbalanced organizational culture):

_____
_____
_____
_____
_____
_____
_____
_____
_____
_____
_____

Key 7: Engage in Self-Care

Progress I have made on this key:

_____
_____
_____
_____
_____
_____
_____
_____
_____
_____
_____
_____
_____
_____
_____
_____
_____
_____

Remaining challenges with this barrier (lack of self-care):

_____
_____
_____
_____
_____
_____
_____
_____
_____
_____
_____

Taking Stock

(see p. 227 in *Your Work, Your Life...Your Way*)

Take some time now to reflect on your current situation. What is your work–life balance satisfaction now?

Today's Date: _____

Your Current Work–Life Balance Satisfaction Level (number between 1 and 10):

How do you feel about this level (in three words or less):

_____

_____

Compare your answers from the first time you completed this exercise (the *Identify Your Current Work–Life Balance Satisfaction* exercise) in the first chapter of this workbook/journal. What is different between now and when you first started reading the book?

_____

_____

_____

_____

_____

_____

_____

_____

_____

_____

_____

_____

_____

_____

_____

_____

Key Reflection

Which keys are you making progress on in terms of putting them into practice?

_____

_____

_____

_____

_____

_____

_____

_____

_____

_____

_____

_____

Which keys and barriers continue to challenge you? Which keys are you having a difficult time putting into practice?

_____

_____

_____

_____

_____

_____

_____

_____

_____

_____

_____

_____

_____

Which barrier(s) are not an issue for you? Which barriers have you addressed to the level you wished to do with the fieldwork?

_____

_____

_____

_____

_____

_____

_____

_____

_____

_____

_____

_____

How will you stay focused on your journey toward a more desired work–life balance? Describe a check-in process that works for you. Remember, it can be on a monthly, quarterly, or semi-annual basis.

_____

_____

_____

_____

_____

_____

_____

_____

_____

_____

_____

_____

_____

Check-In/Check-Up—A New Way of Life
(see p. 232)

This exercise, which parallels the previous *Describe Your Preferred Work–Life Balance Situation* fieldwork (in the *Road Map for the Journey* chapter) and the *Taking Stock* fieldwork (earlier in this chapter), will help you evaluate your current work–life balance satisfaction level at a scheduled time in the future and to assess how it compares to the desired feeling/state/experience you want to be moving toward at that future time. You may want to make several photocopies of this blank fieldwork exercise (or download a free template at *www.7KeysToWorkLifeBalance.com/checkincheckup*) so you can easily reuse it in the coming months and years.

Take some time now to reflect on your current situation. What is your work–life balance satisfaction now?

Today's Date: _____

Your Current Work–Life Balance Satisfaction Level (number between 1 and 10): ☐

How do you feel about this level (in three words or less):

_____

_____

Next, answer the following questions:

How am I feeling about my current state?

_____

_____

_____

_____

_____

_____

_____

_____

What is working well?

_____

_____

_____

_____

_____

_____

_____

_____

What is not working well?

_____

_____

_____

_____

_____

_____

_____

_____

_____

What adjustment(s) can I make to get me closer to my desired work–life balance feeling/state/experience?

Adjustment #1:

_____

_____

_____

_____

Adjustment #2:

_____

_____

_____

_____

Adjustment #3:

_____

_____

_____

_____

Adjustment #4:

_____

_____

_____

_____

Adjustment #5:

_____

_____

_____

_____

Revisiting which key chapters will assist me?

☐	**Key 1 – Develop Priorities**
☐	**Key 2 – Create Boundaries**
☐	**Key 3 – Manage Your Day Efficiently**
☐	**Key 4 – Design Reasonable Expectations**
☐	**Key 5 – Reprioritize Your Values**
☐	**Key 6 – Navigate an Unbalanced Organizational Culture**
☐	**Key 7 – Engage in Self-Care**

Keys to Your Journey

Reflections thus far on my journey toward work–life balance:

Things to remember as I continue on my work–life balance journey:

_____

_____

_____

_____

_____

_____

_____

_____

_____

_____

_____

_____

_____

_____

_____

_____

_____

_____

_____

_____

_____

_____

_____

_____

_____

_____

_____

_____

_____

Don't Forget to Write!

Best wishes on your journey. As you continue to practice using the 7 keys to work–life balance and to overcome the 7 barriers to work–life balance, I would love to hear your progress. Feel free to drop me an e-postcard at *Julie@7KeysToWorkLifeBalance.com.*

About the Author

In ten years as a career and leadership coach, Julie Cohen, PCC, has worked with hundreds of clients to clarify and achieve their professional and personal goals. Whether these clients desired a promotion, better communication skills, more meaning and satisfaction from their work, or improved leadership capabilities, just about all clients wanted to enhance work–life balance. This led Julie to develop "Overcoming the 7 Barriers to Work–Life Balance"—a program that gives participants tools to identify, clarify, and rectify the challenges that they may be facing regarding work–life balance.

Julie brings twenty years of experience in corporate, non-profit, and entrepreneurial entities to her work as a coach. Formerly an internal Executive Coach at Cap Gemini Ernst & Young, LLC, she was part of the design team responsible for developing and implementing a national coaching program for the organization. She is currently coaching Wharton School MBA Candidates as part of a Leadership Development Program along with a wide array of individual and organizational clients around the world.

Julie has a Bachelor of Arts in Economics from the University of Pennsylvania and a Master of Science in Counseling from Villanova University. She is a graduate of Corporate Coach University International's and Coach University's Training Programs, is a past President of the Philadelphia Area Coaches Alliance and a member of the International Coach Federation (ICF). Julie has earned the Professional Certified Coach (PCC) designation from the ICF.

Julie's passion and personal focus on work–life balance evolves as she integrates her roles as business owner, mother, wife, pianist, yoga student, and recycling enthusiast.

For more information or to get in touch with Julie about her coaching services, workshops, and public speaking, visit *www.7KeysToWorkLifeBalance.com* and *www.JulieCohenCoaching.com*.